THE SICKENING HISTORY OF MEDICINE

Plague!

EPIDEMICS AND SCOURGES THROUGH THE AGES

D1036653

J 616.009 Far
Farndon, John
Plague!
WITHDRAWN
$7.99
ocn951563149

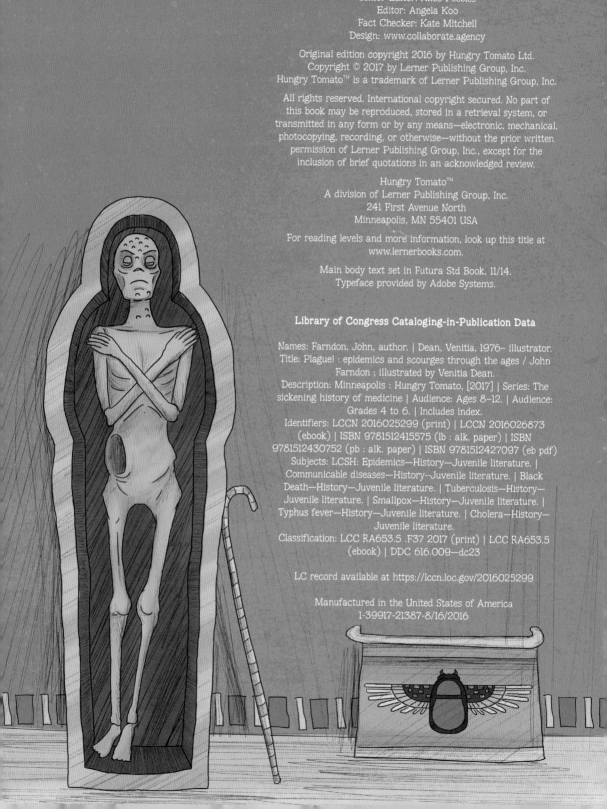

Thanks to the creative team:
Senior Editor: Alice Peebles
Editor: Angela Koo
Fact Checker: Kate Mitchell
Design: www.collaborate.agency

Original edition copyright 2016 by Hungry Tomato Ltd.
Copyright © 2017 by Lerner Publishing Group, Inc.
Hungry Tomato™ is a trademark of Lerner Publishing Group, Inc.

All rights reserved. International copyright secured. No part of
this book may be reproduced, stored in a retrieval system, or
transmitted in any form or by any means—electronic, mechanical,
photocopying, recording, or otherwise—without the prior written
permission of Lerner Publishing Group, Inc., except for the
inclusion of brief quotations in an acknowledged review.

Hungry Tomato™
A division of Lerner Publishing Group, Inc.
241 First Avenue North
Minneapolis, MN 55401 USA

For reading levels and more information, look up this title at
www.lernerbooks.com.

Main body text set in Futura Std Book, 11/14.
Typeface provided by Adobe Systems.

Library of Congress Cataloging-in-Publication Data

Names: Farndon, John, author. | Dean, Venitia, 1976– illustrator.
Title: Plague! : epidemics and scourges through the ages / John
Farndon ; illustrated by Venitia Dean.
Description: Minneapolis : Hungry Tomato, [2017] | Series: The
sickening history of medicine | Audience: Ages 8–12. | Audience:
Grades 4 to 6. | Includes index.
Identifiers: LCCN 2016025299 (print) | LCCN 2016026873
(ebook) | ISBN 9781512415575 (lb : alk. paper) | ISBN
9781512430752 (pb : alk. paper) | ISBN 9781512427097 (eb pdf)
Subjects: LCSH: Epidemics—History—Juvenile literature. |
Communicable diseases—History--Juvenile literature. | Black
Death—History—Juvenile literature. | Tuberculosis—History—
Juvenile literature. | Smallpox—History—Juvenile literature. |
Typhus fever—History—Juvenile literature. | Cholera—History—
Juvenile literature.
Classification: LCC RA653.5 .F37 2017 (print) | LCC RA653.5
(ebook) | DDC 616.009—dc23

LC record available at https://lccn.loc.gov/2016025299

Manufactured in the United States of America
1-39917-21387-8/16/2016

THE SICKENING
HISTORY OF MEDICINE

Plague!

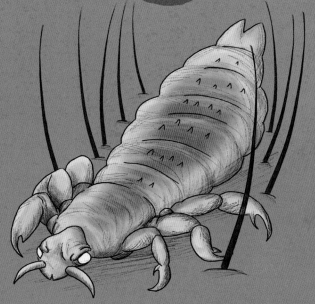

By John Farndon

Illustrated by Venitia Dean

HUNGRY
TOMATO

Contents

INTRODUCTION

It's not nice when you get sick. But if you ever feel sorry for yourself, then this book might just make you feel a little better. In the past, people were battered again and again by horrible diseases that made their skin rot, their hair fall out, their hands turn black, their lungs collapse, and their faces erupt with boils—and that's if they were lucky...

A Happy Ending

Smallpox made life utterly dreadful for English children in the 1700s. Only one out of every three children under the age of three survived it. But smallpox is one of the success stories of modern medicine. Thanks to the discovery of vaccination, it has vanished from the world entirely.

God's Vengeance

One of the frightening things about diseases is that people once had no idea what caused them. Now we know diseases are spread by germs (tiny bacteria and viruses), so we can look for ways to fight them. But in the past there was no explanation. Many people believed diseases were caused by angry gods.

Deadly Rider

In the past, diseases were so devastating that outbreaks were given frightening names, such as plague and pestilence. These names are also given to one of the four horsemen of the apocalypse—four terrifying riders who, according to the Christian Bible, will descend on the world on its final day of judgment.

The Worst Outbreaks

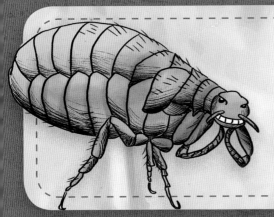

Modern doctors call the worst outbreaks of disease *pandemics*. These spread far and wide, killing millions. Throughout history there have been many pandemics. One of the worst was the Black Death of 1346–1353, carried by fleas, which killed 75–200 million people worldwide.

It's the Pits

It's hard to imagine just how bad outbreaks of disease were in the past. In many cities during the Black Death, there were too few people left to bury those who died. Bodies would be chucked into pits and left to rot.

THE OLDEST KILLER

Malaria is a really terrible disease that affects mostly tropical regions. It kills nearly half a million people every year and makes over 200 million ill. People become infected when a mosquito bite injects a tiny microbe into their blood.

Tiny Assassin

Malaria is caused by the microbe called plasmodium. But it is spread by female *Anopheles* mosquitoes. When this mosquito bites someone infected with the disease to feed on their blood, it picks up the microbe. When it bites someone else, it passes on the microbe, infecting them with malaria.

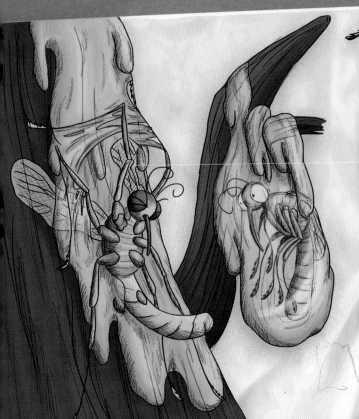

An Ancient Disease

Malaria is the oldest known disease. The plasmodium microbes that cause it have been found in mosquitoes from as long ago as 30 million years. These mosquitoes were trapped in the resin that oozes from some trees, then perfectly preserved as the resin hardened and turned to amber.

Fever Tree

Malaria was spread to the Americas by European settlers in the 1500s. But the American Indians learned to treat it using the powdered bark of the cinchona tree, which soon became known as the "fever tree." A drug called quinine, which is made from cinchona bark, is still an effective way of treating malaria.

Bad Air

The word *malaria* comes from the Latin for "bad air," and for a long time people thought it was caused by the damp, smelly air given off by swamps. They weren't so wrong because these swamps are the perfect breeding ground for the mosquitoes that pass on the disease.

Smelly Breath

Malaria became a killer disease when people first settled down to farm. The people who built the Egyptian pyramids stuffed themselves with garlic to ward off the disease. They must have had very smelly breath! But scientists think garlic really does help fight malaria.

DEADLY BLISTERS

In 541–542 CE, the city of Constantinople (now Istanbul) was utterly ravaged by an outbreak of a terrible disease called the Justinian plague, named after the city's ruler, Justinian. Up to ten thousand people died each day, and the streets were piled high with bodies.

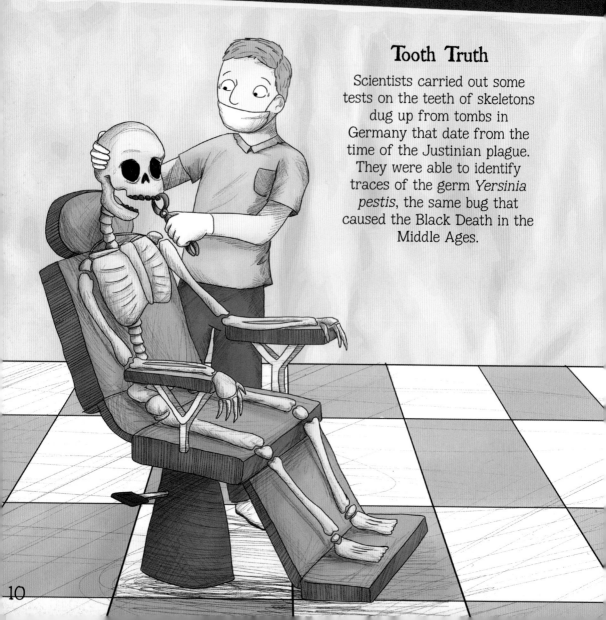

Tooth Truth

Scientists carried out some tests on the teeth of skeletons dug up from tombs in Germany that date from the time of the Justinian plague. They were able to identify traces of the germ *Yersinia pestis*, the same bug that caused the Black Death in the Middle Ages.

Looking Good (Not!)

If someone caught the plague, they would feel like they had the worst flu ever. Then parts of their body would turn black, and their skin would erupt with terrible pus-filled swellings called buboes—or worse still, their lungs would dissolve from the inside. Within a week they'd be dead.

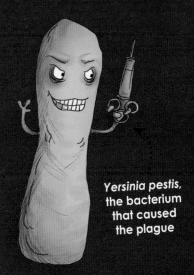

Yersinia pestis, the bacterium that caused the plague

That Pesky *Pestis*

Rats may have carried the disease to Constantinople, but the culprit was really a tiny bacterium called *Yersinia pestis. Yersinia* may be tiny, but it was one of the deadliest killers in history. It also brought the Black Death in the Middle Ages and a plague that killed millions in Asia in the later 1800s.

The March of Death

The plague germs were carried to Constantinople by rats that stowed away on ships carrying grain from Egypt. From Constantinople, the plague spread rapidly, engulfing most of North Africa, the Middle East, and Europe. Altogether, it is thought to have killed 25 million people in less than two years.

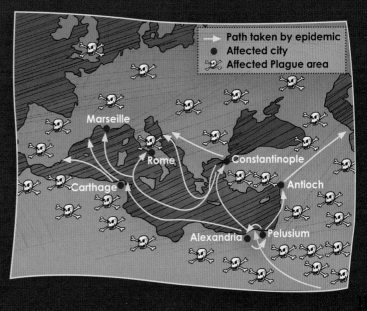

- → Path taken by epidemic
- ● Affected city
- ☠ Affected Plague area

Marseille

Rome

Constantinople

Antioch

Carthage

Alexandria   Pelusium

THE BLACK DEATH

No disease has ever been quite so terrifying and deadly as the Black Death. It killed up to 200 million people around the world between 1346 and 1353. In some places, whole towns and villages were wiped out, and there was no one left to bury the dead.

The Pied Piper

According to legend, the town of Hamelin in Germany was infested by rats. The town hired a piper to lure the rats out of the city to drown in the river and save the city from plague. But the mayor of the town, the legend says, didn't pay the piper for his work, so the piper lured the town's children away too...

Dance of Death

After the plague, the shadow of death hung heavily over the people of the Middle Ages, and it became a key theme in art of the time. Many artists drew pictures of the *Danse Macabre*, or "Dance of Death," in which the dead invited people from all walks of life to dance on a grave, showing how death comes to all.

Mass Burial

So many people died so quickly that the streets were piled with corpses, and the smell of rotting flesh was terrible. There were so many bodies to dispose of that the survivors just dug large trenches and piled them in one on top of the other, then covered them over with dirt.

Don't Blame the Rats

The Black Death was probably the bubonic plague, a horrible disease caused by the bacterium *Yersinia pestis*. In the 1600s people thought it was passed to humans by black rats. But scientists think the disease may have first come from gerbils, not rats.

Plague out of the East

The plague may have started in central Asia and spread west. It reached Europe when Mongol armies catapulted infected corpses into the city of Kaffa in Crimea as they besieged it in 1347. Genoese traders trapped in the city fled, carrying the infection with them to Europe.

THE GREAT PLAGUE

The Black Death was the worst outbreak of disease in history. But for more than three centuries after, Europe was subjected to repeated plagues. The last massive outbreak was the Great Plague, which struck London in 1665.

Doctor Beak

It was a brave doctor who dared to go near plague victims to tend to them. Because the disease was thought to be spread by bad air, some doctors dressed in a weird costume with a face mask and a long beak filled with herbs and flowers. They thought these might keep the bad air away.

Pneumonic plague

Wild Flea Hosts

Urban and Household Hosts

Dog

Prairie dog

Flea

Gerbil

Flea to black rat

Black rat to flea

Plague Pathway

Bubonic plague is caused by a bacterium that infects humans when they are bitten by a flea. These fleas live on rats. They can live on cats and dogs too. Bubonic plague can then develop into pneumonic plague, which dissolves the lungs horribly and can be spread through the air in coughs and sneezes.

Little Monsters

The *Yersinia pestis* bacterium that caused the bubonic plague was carried by fleas. But pneumonic plague could be spread from one human to another through the air. The Black Death and Great Plague were probably a mix of both kinds.

Stinky Streets

In the seventeenth century, there were no drains in cities like London, and people just threw the contents of their toilets out into ditches in the narrow streets—often barely missing people walking past! In these conditions, infections of all kinds could spread easily.

THE WHITE PLAGUE

Bubonic plague is now, thankfully, mostly a terror of the past. But the horrible lung disease tuberculosis, or TB, once known as the white plague, is still with us, and millions of people around the world are affected by it.

Trust me, I'm an Emperor...

The mythical Chinese Yellow Emperor, Huangdi, fancied himself a doctor. A medical book called the *Huangdi Neijing*, said to be based on his ideas, contains the earliest known description of TB. But it was written over two thousand years after Huangdi's time, so someone must have had a very good memory!

Touch Me, Touch Me!

TB doesn't just affect the lungs. It can cause swellings on the neck called scrofula. In the Middle Ages, people with scrofula would line up to see the king because it was thought that being touched by the king would cure them. The disease became known as the King's Evil.

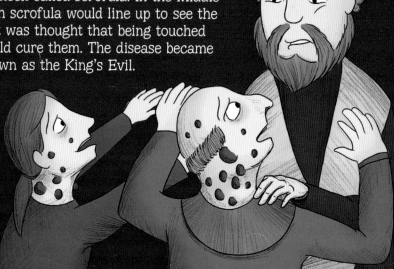

Symptoms of Tuberculosis

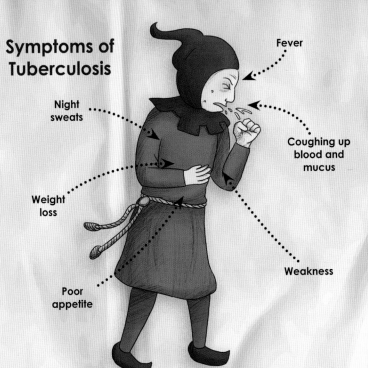

Fever

Night sweats

Coughing up blood and mucus

Weight loss

Weakness

Poor appetite

Coughs and Fever

TB is a horrible disease that kills people slowly if they are not treated. It makes people cough terribly, often spitting up blood. It makes them sweat badly at night. And it makes them lose a lot of weight and become weak, which is why it came to be called consumption—it seemed to consume the victim's body.

Vampire Killers

People once thought TB victims had pale skin because vampires were sucking their blood and draining their lives away. That's why, when so many young girls died of consumption in the 1800s, writers wrote horror stories about vampire attacks.

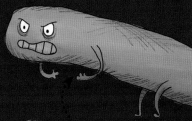

The *Mycobacterium tuberculosis* (MTB) bacterium, which causes TB

Romantic Death?

In the 1800s, consumption claimed the lives of many young girls and poets such as John Keats. Their pale skin, for some, had "a terrible beauty." And so the disease came to seem almost romantic. But the victims suffered terribly, and their deaths caused their loved ones great heartache.

17

THE POX

Thanks to vaccination, the disease smallpox is dead. But for a long time in the past, it was the world's worst killer. Even those who survived usually ended up with faces horribly disfigured by the skin rash it caused.

Mummy, I'm Sick

The Egyptians usually preserved the bodies of their pharaohs (kings) after they died by mummifying them. That is why we are able to see the terrible marks of smallpox on the face of the young pharaoh Ramesses V's mummy, more than three thousand years after he died from the disease.

Nasty Virus

Smallpox is caused by a virus called *Variola*. It jumped from rodents to humans 16,000 years ago and learned how to invade body cells, causing smallpox. Thanks to vaccination, there are now just a few *variola* viruses left—safely locked up!

White Queen

In October 1562, the young Elizabeth I of England caught smallpox. For a week her life hung in the balance. She pulled through, but her face was scarred by the disease, and her hair fell out. For the rest of her life, she painted her face in thick white lead paint and egg whites and wore wigs.

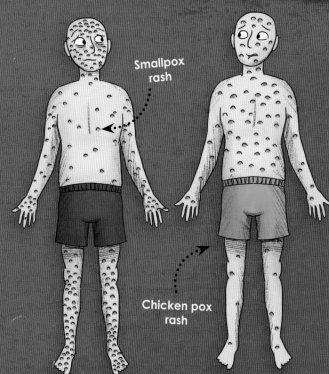

Smallpox rash

Chicken pox rash

Signs of Smallpox

For two weeks after a person catches the smallpox virus, nothing happens. Then they start to feel like they have flu, but they seem to get better. Suddenly red spots appear on their faces and forearms before spreading over their whole body, and they become very ill. Smallpox can look like mild chicken pox, but the marks are much denser.

NAPOLEON'S NIGHTMARE

Like smallpox, typhus has been almost eliminated, thanks to vaccination. But typhus was once a deadly disease that brought a great deal of suffering and death. At first, victims suffered from an illness like flu, then developed a terrible rash over their whole body.

Beaten by a Microbe

The French emperor Napoleon conquered most of Europe. But after reaching Moscow, Russia, in 1812 and finding it abandoned, he decided to retreat. On the way back, through a bitter winter, more of his army was killed by typhus than by all the armies of Russia.

Nasty Bugs

Typhus is caused by various kinds of bacteria called *Rickettsia*. They infect humans either through animal droppings or nasty little lice and fleas. These can make people itch so much that they scratch their skin and make an opening for the bacteria.

20

Delousing

In the aftermath of World War II, typhus could easily have spread rapidly among closely packed soldiers and the hordes of refugees. But millions of lives were saved when people were sprayed with the newly discovered chemical DDT, which killed the lice carrying the disease.

Sentenced to Sickness

In the 1500s, many crime suspects died in prison of typhus or "jail fever" before they could be tried. In 1586, thirty-eight fishermen accused of stealing fish went to court in Exeter, England. They were half dead of typhus—and they spread the disease to all the court officials!

Irish Fever

The poor in Ireland suffered especially from typhus at the time of the Irish famine in the 1840s. Many starved, and just as many were forced to leave their homes for other countries when a disease killed off the potatoes that they relied on for food. From Ireland, typhus spread to England and became known as Irish fever.

21

CHOLERA

Cholera is one of the nastiest diseases there is, giving people diarrhea and making them horribly sick. People become infected by drinking dirty water in which the bacterium *Vibrio cholerae* thrives.

New Sewers

Sewage was often collected in tanks called cesspits or dumped in the river, which made London super smelly. After doctor John Snow discovered the dangers of sewage contamination (*opposite*), London embarked on a massive program of building drains to wash sewage away. Few people got cholera in the city ever again.

Snow's Discovery

No one knew what caused cholera until an outbreak of the disease in London's Soho in 1854 prompted John Snow to investigate. Snow found that victims had all drunk water from a pump on Broadwick Street. The pump water was being contaminated by leaking sewage.

Cholera Calling

The *Vibrio cholerae* bacterium that causes cholera thrives in water and food that has been contaminated by human waste. Humans can get cholera if they eat sea creatures that swim in sewage-contaminated water. When people eat or drink anything containing cholera germs, the germs multiply in the gut and cause serious illness.

Flying the Yellow Flag

Cholera became widespread in the nineteenth century when towns grew, yet people had poor access to fresh water and had poor sewage systems. If anyone aboard a ship came down with cholera, the ship had to fly a yellow-and-black flag to warn other ships. No one from the ship would be allowed ashore for a month.

YELLOW FEVER

Yellow fever is a dangerous tropical disease that makes people very ill with fever and vomiting. Sometimes it makes the skin turn yellow as the germs damage the cells of the liver.

Yellow for Danger

In most cases, yellow fever only makes people sweaty and sick for a few days. But for one in six people, the virus then attacks the liver, making the skin turn yellow and causing a nasty abdominal pain. Then the mouth and eyes bleed, and so does the gut, making the sufferer vomit black blood.

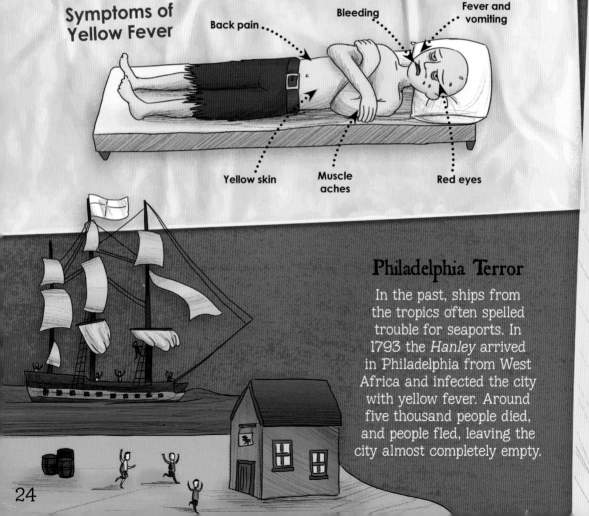

Symptoms of Yellow Fever

Back pain · · · · · · ·

Bleeding · · · · · ·

Fever and vomiting

Yellow skin

Muscle aches

Red eyes

Philadelphia Terror

In the past, ships from the tropics often spelled trouble for seaports. In 1793 the *Hanley* arrived in Philadelphia from West Africa and infected the city with yellow fever. Around five thousand people died, and people fled, leaving the city almost completely empty.

Who'll Nurse the Sick?

African American women were often hired as nurses during yellow fever epidemics because people wrongly believed that they were immune to yellow fever. That was how Mary Mahoney became the first trained African American nurse in the United States in 1879.

Deadly Mosquito

Yellow fever is a virus spread by the bite of the female mosquito *Aedes egypti*. If this mosquito has bitten an infected person, the next time it sucks someone's blood, it injects its saliva into the wound along with the deadly virus. *Aedes egypti* can spread Zika fever and dengue fever in the same way.

It's the Mosquitoes!

People once thought yellow fever spread from person to person through the air. But in 1881, a Cuban doctor named Carlos Finlay showed that the pesky little mosquito was to blame. People learned that it was important to avoid areas with mosquitoes and to sleep with mosquito nets at night.

SPANISH FLU

Most of the time, flu is just a minor winter illness. But some forms are deadly killers. An outbreak of one particular kind called Spanish flu killed between 50 and 100 million people in 1918–1919, making it the deadliest disaster ever.

Swine Flu

Pigs also suffered from the flu outbreak in 1918. Some say they caught it from humans, and others say the pigs gave it to us. Ever since, people have been worried that variations of flu that develop in pigs and birds might pass to humans and cause another outbreak as bad as Spanish flu.

Flu in the Trenches

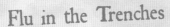

In World War I, millions of soldiers were crowded together in muddy trenches in France. Pigs were crammed up near them too, to provide food. It's thought that the flu virus developed its deadly form as it was passed back and forth between pigs and soldiers.

Sprayed in Snot

Flu is very contagious, or easily spread. Someone with flu only has to sneeze for tiny droplets full of the virus to spray into the air and for someone else to breathe them in. During serious flu outbreaks, people may wear masks to avoid breathing in germs—but they are not very effective.

Camp Funston

Camp Funston might sound like a nice place to go on vacation. But in March 1918 it was anything but. It was a training camp for young soldiers in Kansas, and it is thought to be where the terrible Spanish flu epidemic began.

TERRIBLE TIMES

Thankfully most outbreaks of disease come to an end—when they run out of victims or when victims recover. But they cause a lot of suffering. Here are some of history's worst.

541-542 CE
Justinian Plague

This plague (probably bubonic) spread out from Constantinople (modern Istanbul) and killed up to half of the world's population.

400 BCE

600 CE

430 BCE
Plague of Athens

Ancient Athens was once very powerful—until it was hit by a terrible outbreak of disease, which experts believe may have been typhus.

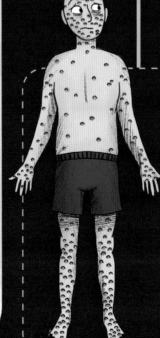

165-180 CE
Antonine Plague

In 165 CE the Roman Empire was ravaged by a pandemic that killed 5 million people and fatally weakened the power of Rome. Experts think it might have been smallpox or measles.

1665-1666
Great Plague of London

The plague kept coming back, but the Great Plague was the last major outbreak, killing one hundred thousand people in London—a fifth of the city's entire population.

1918-1919 Spanish Flu

Immediately after World War I, the world was hit by the worst-ever outbreak of flu, called the Spanish flu. It infected one in three people around the world and killed up to 100 million.

1855 - Third Plague

Following the Justinian plague and the Black Death, there was a third great pandemic of plague. It began in China in 1855 and swept through India to reach the Americas.

1700

1900

1346-1353 Black Death

This was one of the most terrifying pandemics ever. It killed 30 million people in Europe—a third of the population—in just six years.

Twentieth Century Smallpox

Before it was finally eliminated in 1979, smallpox killed up to half a billion people in the world during the twentieth century. It was perhaps the worst killer ever. Thank goodness it is no more!

GRUESOME SYMPTOMS

Epidermodysplasia verruciformis is a very rare disease that makes giant warts grow thickly all over the body.

Buboes are horrible pus-filled blisters that erupt under the arms or on the neck or groin. They are a sign of bubonic plague.

A single sneeze can spray out 6 million little viruses into the world.

If a person was bitten by a dog with rabies, they might start dribbling and foaming at the mouth with saliva.

If someone throws up, their vomit often seems to contain carrots, even if they haven't eaten any! These are actually parts of the stomach lining that have come off.

Leprosy has such terrible effects on the body that those who suffered from the disease were once cut off from other people and forced to live in leper colonies.

GLOSSARY

amber resin that oozed from trees long ago and turned solid

bacterium a tiny living thing made from just a single living cell. A small number of them cause disease. *Bacteria* is the plural of *bacterium*.

Black Death the terrible pandemic of bubonic plague that swept through the world in the 1340s, killing millions

bubo a huge boil-like eruption on the skin caused by bubonic plague

bubonic plague a dreadful disease cause by the *Yersinia pestis* bacterium that often causes buboes

consumption the old name for the killer lung disease tuberculosis

epidemic a widespread outbreak of an infectious disease

malaria a tropical disease spread by mosquitoes

microbe a microscopic living thing, especially one that causes diseases

pandemic a huge worldwide outbreak of an infectious disease

plague a really bad epidemic, or the name for the disease spread by the *Yersinia pestis* germ

plasmodium a tiny organism that causes the disease malaria

pneumonic plague a dreadful disease related to bubonic plague that affects the lungs rather than causing buboes

vaccination the use of dead or inactive germs to stimulate the immune system to guard against infection

virus a tiny germ that reproduces only inside other living cells—including yours

white plague a disease, usually tuberculosos, that makes the skin pale

Harris County Public Library
Houston, Texas

Index

The Author

John Farndon is the author of many books on science, technology, and nature, including the international best sellers *Do Not Open* and *Do You Think You're Clever?* He has been shortlisted five times for the Royal Society's Young People's Book Prize for a science book.

The Illustrator

Venitia Dean grew up in Brighton, in the United Kingdom. She has loved drawing ever since she could hold a pencil. After receiving a digital drawing tablet for her nineteenth birthday, she began working digitally. She hasn't looked back since!